Heaven Vs Reincarnation

Dharma

Clink Street

London | New York

Published by Clink Street Publishing 2018

Copyright © 2018

First edition.

ISBN:

978-1-912850-33-4 - colour paperback

978-1-912850-31-0 - paperback

978-1-912850-32-7 - ebook

Preface

This book is a small cartoon-based version of my book in text - "Heaven Vs Reincarnation" by Dharma

As they say, a picture is worth a 1,000 words and I am hoping that by using some cartoons, I can get my point across forcefully.

Our views on God and religion have been stuck in the past. We continue to regurgitate old ideas written in ancient times without questioning such ideas. Just because a book is written a 1,000 or 2,000 years ago does not mean the people, at that time, had some special insight nor does it mean that God walked this earth around that time.

The ancients were not bad people . They simply wrote down what they thought was right, they put forth their view of God, heavily influenced by the life they had at that time. Brutal Kings/ Dictators and strong men ruled, demanding obedience and loyalty in return for their favors. That was the template for God, at least for Christianity and Islam, the dominant religions of today.

Get down on our knees, beg for mercy, swear loyalty to the King and be rewarded, that was the life then and those were the ideas that were written down and sadly, the vast majority of humanity still blindly follows such ideas even today and even though life today is vastly different.

Through my books, I hope to change the conversation, infuse fresh ideas on religion and spirituality.

You can reach out to me at: HeavenVsReincarnation@Yahoo.com

Careful what you wish for, it will come true

First, I want to make it clear that Hindu ideas were not intended just for Hindus. The correct name for Hinduism is Sanatana Dharma, loosely translated to Eternal Truth. What kind of a name is that for a religion? Exactly! This faith started with some enlightened sages imparting knowledge to those around them in ancient India. Their ideas were for everyone.

The cartoon tells us that if all we wish for is the easy lazy life of doing nothing, having zero worries or responsibilities, then certainly our wishes will come true but not the way we intended them to turn out. Everyone has heard of Hindus talking about coming back as animals or bugs - well, this concept has been much misunderstood. It was seen as a punishment for criminal acts in a previous life and that is the wrong view. One will simply attain the life that one wishes for, that's all - Tat Tvam Asi.

Through life, God has taught us that all life gets to live in relative comfort and in the nest for only a short period of our lives. We all have to grow up and face the world on our own, stand on our own two feet and make a living. To wish for a lazy life, a life spent in useless existence of eternal dependency, eternal childhood is wrong and goes against God's laws.

But such wishes will come true. As a tree or a pet, a cat, a dog or a pig. Such people will be well taken care of, nothing to do except, eat, poop and sleep, with zero worries and responsibilities! That cat is in Heaven!

"Heaven Vs Reincarnation"
Book by Dharma

3 Ways to End Pain and Suffering

The quickest way to end any problems is, of course, just run away from it and that is what Heaven accomplishes. Just run away from life's problems and hide. Give no thought to your loved ones still down here or for that matter anyone else. Did you spend your time helping at a homeless shelter? Now, it's someone else's problem. Did you use your time to work for a cure for cancer? Not your problem anymore. Is your country at war? Did you die fighting the enemy? Now, no longer your concern!

Heaven appeals to the coward, the weak and religions exploit it by making cheap promises of magic lands in the sky where the living will be easy, provided we join their religion of course! And yet even the brightest among us fail to see this ponzi-scheme for what it really is.

The second quickest way to end pain and suffering is never to have any desires, that way we will never know the pain of failure. Never try anything, never fail at anything, never have to feel any pain. Such ideas appeal again to the weak, the old at heart, such ideas are not for the strong, the young, or the dreamer.

The best way to end pain and suffering is to face it squarely. Problems need to be faced and fought. We will get knocked down, plenty of times, but the strong and the warrior does not give up. God needs you down here, the strong and the warrior belong here down on earth.

3 WAYS TO END PAIN AND SUFFERING

RUN AWAY FROM TROUBLE, FROM PAIN AND SUFFERING – THAT IS THE **QUICKEST WAY** TO END PAIN AND SUFFERING

BACK DOOR

HEAVEN

DEATH!

I WANT NOTHING, I DESIRE NOTHING. **DESIRES ARE THE ROOT OF ALL PAIN AND SUFFERING** AND NOW, AFTER HAVING GIVEN UP ALL DESIRES, I AM HAPPY AND AT PEACE!

AND YOU HAVE ALSO GIVEN UP ON LIFE. **YOU DESIRE NOTHING, NOTHING IS WHAT YOU WILL GET.**

ARE YOU **TOUGH ENOUGH** FOR LIFE? LIFE WILL KNOCK YOU DOWN, BUT YOU MUST GET UP! FACE YOUR PROBLEMS, FIGHT THEM. END POVERTY, DISEASE, CLIMATE CHANGE, TERRORISM, DISCRIMINATION, ANIMAL AND CHILD ABUSE! MAKE GOD PROUD!

FRONT DOOR

REINCARNATION

LIFE, REAL LIFE!

What Does One DO in Heaven?

What is incredible, is that such a question has never been asked! NEVER! EVER! In all the annals of human history, such a question has never been posed to a theist leader spouting about the after-life! Not one person has ever asked - "ok, we get there, it's all wonderful, peaches and cream, but what do we do on a daily basis? Is there any work to do? What kind of work would the being that created this huge universe might have for us puny humans? With one thought, She can create trillions of robots that can work night and day! How are we of any use? So then, do we just sit or float around staring at each other? Or will we snore away eternity? Is this the 'Grand Plan of God'?"

If you were told that in a few days you will be shipped off to another country, as an adult, would not your first thought be, "How will I be able to support myself? What kind of jobs will be available for my skill set?" Aren't these the thoughts that go through your mind? They MUST, right? And yet, when it comes to Heaven, it seems everyone simply expects God to nicely cater to their comforts? Think of it - even your own mother will not let you do that! Even your own parents will tell you to go out and get a job! And we are supposed to believe that this being will nicely nursemaid you for eternity? Ah, the brainwashing power of religion! Even the best of us are not immune it seems.

THE ONE QUESTION THAT DESTROYS HEAVEN

I GET IT - HEAVEN WILL BE ALL WONDERFUL AND JOYOUS AND EVERYTHING, BUT **WHAT DOES ONE DO IN HEAVEN**, ANYWAY? ANY TYPE OF WORK? WHAT WORK WOULD THE MAKER OF THIS UNIVERSE MIGHT HAVE FOR US LOWLY AND WEAK HUMAN BEINGS?

THE **EASY, LAZY LIFE** OF A FREELOADER FOR ETERNITY? A USELESS LIFE FOR ETERNITY?

GOD IS RUNNING **FACTORIES** UP IN HEAVEN? GOODS TO BE EXPORTED WHERE? GOD NEEDS MONEY?

NEITHER ANSWER MAKES SENSE. BUT FORTUNATELY FOR US **NO ONE EVER ASKS US ANY UNCOMFORTABLE QUESTIONS.** NOT THE MEDIA, NOT THE EDUCATED, NOR THE PHILOSOPHERS & TEACHERS. ESPECIALLY NONE FROM THE GREEDY BELIEVERS WHO SEE GOD AS THEIR TICKET TO THE EASY, LAZY GOOD LIFE. ALL WE GET ARE FLUFF QUESTIONS LIKE **"WHAT WILL HEAVEN BE LIKE?"**. AND WE CAN TALK ABOUT HOW WONDERFUL IT WILL BE AND THAT MAKES THEM SO HAPPY! **EVEN THE BEST OF MINDS, SO EASILY BRAINWASHED!**

Are you the Savior or the Saved?

What are you, the damsel in distress or the knight in shining armor? The coward safely tucked under the bed or the warrior in the middle of battle?

Way too many shootings, right? Way too many school shootings taking innocent lives. On February 14, 2018 in Parkland, Florida, at M.S. Douglas High School, a macabre shooting happened, innocents were killed. Most ran away but a few risked their lives to save the children. Football coach Aaron Feis died trying to save innocent lives. Anthony Borges, just a kid, helped hide other students and suffered 5 gun shots!

It is not wrong to run away when lives are threatened? But it takes a special human being to put his or her life on the line for others. To make God proud is not easy, let's say that again - to make God proud will not be easy. Have you ever heard any religious leader use such words? No, they are too busy helping you run away to Heaven.

Life teaches us that nothing good comes easy. What does that tell you about Heaven? All you have to do is join a religion and pray to a particular God and you will be rewarded? Like a Dictator rewarding his loyal supporters? Is God no better? The pain is here and the suffering is here, this is where you are needed. God needs you down here.

The pain is here, suffering is here! This is where you are needed. God needs you down here.

"HEAVEN VS REINCARNATION" BY DHARMA
ORDER ONLINE FROM BOOKSELLERS

HEAVEN	REINCARNATION
THE WOMB, CHILDHOOD, THE PAST, COWARD, FLEE, SELFISH, RETIRE, OLD, EXIST, **WEAK**, SHAMELESS, TAKER, **SAVED**, ANIMAL, BEG, HAND-OUT, FOOLISH, LOWER, JOY AND HAPPINESS, FANTASY	LIFE, ADULTHOOD, THE FUTURE, WARRIOR, FIGHT, CARING, ASPIRE, YOUNG, LIVE, **STRONG**, SELF-RESPECT, GIVER, **SAVIOR**, HUMAN, EARN, HAND-UP, WISE, HIGHER, PAIN AND SUFFERING, REAL LIFE!

Heaven is a Metaphor for the Womb, Childhood & the Past, Whereas Reincarnation stands for Life, Adulthood and the Future

There is and has never been any evidence for God, the Heavens and Hells and Reincarnation. So if such places and events are non-existent, we must conclude that they are but ideas and imaginations. Heaven then stands for the womb, childhood and the past, whereas Reincarnation stands for Life, adulthood and the future.

Think for a moment what you have been told what Heaven would be like? Does it not resemble your Childhood? Care-free days spent playing, having few worries, knowing that you are loved, protected and cared for? Someone who will look out for you, keep you safe and happy?

Heaven is the yearning for those days of the past, in childhood as well as in the womb, we were happy and content. But then suddenly, we were brutally thrown out of this Eden into a cold, hard world! We start crying almost instantly because for the first time we felt pain! And that is how life starts! Life comes pre-packaged with pain and suffering. To wish for a life without pain and suffering is to wish for death and/or to remain the unborn.

In the picture below we see a young man setting out into the world. But why? Why not stay in the nest? Parents will provide, keep him safe and cater to his needs. But without venturing out, this young man will never start his life. All creatures know this law and obey this law. To think one can run back into the womb, stay a child forever is sheer foolishness. You can't live in the past, you have to move forward into the future.

"Heaven Vs Reincarnation"
By Dharma

Heaven
The Womb, Childhood, the Past, Coward, Flee, Selfish, Retire, Exist, Weak, Taker, Saved, Animal, Beg, Hand-Out, Foolish, Lower, Joy and Happiness, Fantasy.

Reincarnation
Life, Adulthood, the Future, Warrior, Fight, Caring, Work, Live, Strong, Giver, Savior, Human, Earn, Hand-Up, Wise, Higher, Pain and Suffering, REAL LIFE!

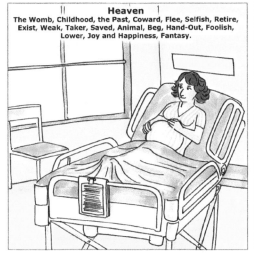

No Theists When Death Comes Calling

You have all heard of "No Atheists in Fox-holes" - basically poking fun at Atheists, saying that when they are afraid for their life, they will call out for help from the deity they don't believe in. Well, funny thing is that I see Theists not being too happy either when death comes calling. That is a surprise, right? Life is a sin, God is waiting, death has come to whisk them off to Heaven, a place of eternal joy and happiness! Wow! No more worries or responsibilities. It is fun, fun, fun each and every day!

And here is death coming to take them to such a wonderful place and surprise, Theists DON'T WANT TO GO! What? God is waiting, Heaven is waiting, all that wonderful world is waiting, they get to get away from this awful horrible life and they don't want to go? They go to Heaven, kicking and screaming, clawing and biting, clinging to life with every fibre of their being. Does that make any sense at all?

Have you ever heard of anyone throwing a party to celebrate their cancer diagnosis? When the doc tells them that they have but a few more months to live? Why is that? Suddenly they want to live, they are suddenly enlightened, suddenly they realize life for the gift that it is. Yes, life is a gift from God and God will continue to bestow this gift on you as long as you want it. Those who chase after Heaven are chasing after 'Fool's Gold'.

"HeavenVsReincarnation" by Dharma

Coward Or Warrior?

Sadly, gun violence and death has become commonplace here in the US. There was one in Las Vegas where a deranged man sat down in his hotel room overlooking a concert and let loose mayhem with his cache of guns! Hundreds of innocents died that day. When we hear about such events, we get sick of life, we understand that life is no picnic and we wish for a nicer, calmer life. Religions take advantage and make easy promises of the easy life. To be had elsewhere, but first we must join their religion, but of course.

Sadly, even the best of us fail to see through the Ponzi-scheme at play here. The likes of Bernie Madoff use the same tactics as religion does and have been very successful at it.

But in life nothing comes without a cost - there is no free lunch. God has taught us that through life. Life's lessons are God's lessons. Those running away from life end up as lower life forms. They get their wish. They get to be who they are (Tat Tvam Asi) or what they want. Life is definitely easier for our pet cat, dog, turtle or even a pig.

Reincarnation is not for everybody. It is for the warrior in all of us. Those who realize that the good things in life are earned, never given nor begged for. We will face all that life can throw at us and yet push forward. Running away is not the answer to life's problems. Well, it is for the coward, but then the coward cares little for others. All his thoughts are for his own well-being.

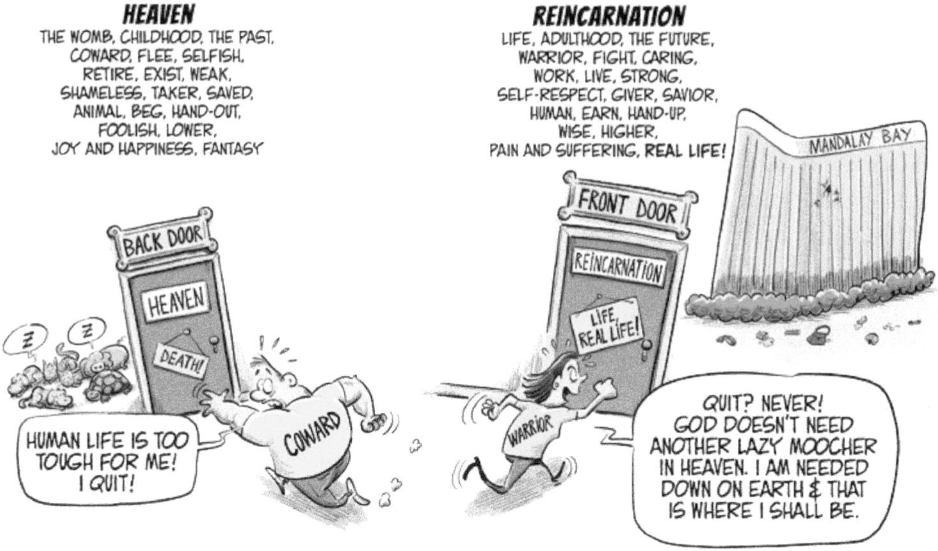
HEAVEN
THE WOMB, CHILDHOOD, THE PAST, COWARD, FLEE, SELFISH, RETIRE, EXIST, WEAK, SHAMELESS, TAKER, SAVED, ANIMAL, BEG, HAND-OUT, FOOLISH, LOWER, JOY AND HAPPINESS, FANTASY
REINCARNATION
LIFE, ADULTHOOD, THE FUTURE, WARRIOR, FIGHT, CARING, WORK, LIVE, STRONG, SELF-RESPECT, GIVER, SAVIOR, HUMAN, EARN, HAND-UP, WISE, HIGHER, PAIN AND SUFFERING, REAL LIFE!
MANDALAY BAY
BACK DOOR
HEAVEN
DEATH!
FRONT DOOR
REINCARNATION
LIFE, REAL LIFE!
COWARD
WARRIOR
HUMAN LIFE IS TOO TOUGH FOR ME! I QUIT!
QUIT? NEVER! GOD DOESN'T NEED ANOTHER LAZY MOOCHER IN HEAVEN. I AM NEEDED DOWN ON EARTH & THAT IS WHERE I SHALL BE.

Religious Brain washing

There is no other word for it, brainwashing is the right word. When people kill in the name of religion, we have to conclude that there is something seriously wrong with some religious teachings and its followers. As the cartoon shows, religion completely contradicts all the morals and ethics we instill in our kids. We tell them that there is no free lunch, that nothing good comes without hard work and effort. That if something is being given away for free it must be worthless. To not take what is not earned. If the teacher makes a mistake and gives your kid higher marks or grades, and if he/she spoke up, would you not be proud of your child? Can you imagine the teacher changing an F to a D just because the student cried and begged?

Yet when it comes to religious promises all our morals and ethics go out of the window it seems. Now it is ok to have free lunches and dinners for eternity. Now it is ok for actions not to matter, one's worth decided by one's religious affiliation. Be denied for a job or a promotion because of your religion? That is plain wrong, isn't it? But "God" does that every day? "God" has one simple rule, he divides people based on religion? All that you did in life does not matter? Morals don't matter, ethics don't matter, Individuality does not matter? Pedophiles, mass murderers, rapists believers get rewarded while the Gandhijis, Einsteins, the Buddhas of the world get hell?

And all it took was some sweet promises of the easy good life for people to sell their souls. Brainwashing as it finest.

"HEAVEN VS REINCARNATION" BY DHARMA

The Dichotomy of the Minority and Majority

A strange facet of human nature is how quickly we change our views depending on which side we are on. As a minority we are wonderfully enlightened, we use words like, "we are all human beings, we are all the same, if cut, do we not all bleed? We all have loved ones, we all have hopes, dreams and aspirations just like everyone else". If it is a religious minority facing discrimination, it is. "We must not see religion, we must see people" etc etc - all very true and wonderful words.

But something strange happens once we gain in numbers or become the majority. Then suddenly all the good words go out of the window it seems. I was told by my African-American "friend" that I was headed for Hell. Yes, the very same person who would get heated when facing discrimination based on his skin color, will get angry and upset if followed around in a store and yet turns around and tells me that I will be set apart and sent to gas chambers in Hell simply because I did not share his beliefs. I am to be discriminated based on my beliefs and he was "ok"with that.

What a quick change! What would account for his changed behavior? He went from being a minority , an African-American colored person living as a minority in a white society. To being a Christian and now a member of the majority! His perspective immediately changed! The top part of the cartoon depicts the Oscar-Awards show of a few years ago when the presenter views changed while commenting on another race.

"Heaven Vs Reincarnation"
By Dharma

Ask not what God can do for you, but what you can do for God!

Ok, I took some liberties with the slogan but you get the idea. So many are wrapped up in what God can do for them. They want to get away from the harshness of life, life is hard, they hope for an easy lazy life and religions are more than happy to exploit that concept. God created only one world, this one, it is the religions who came up with fantasy lands in the sky where the living is easy.

The coward runs away from life, the warrior embraces it. When the coward looks at the enemy, all he can think of is his own well-being. How he will be hurt, how he might get injured or die and all his thoughts are about himself. Whereas when the warrior looks at the enemy, he realizes that without him, his family's welfare is at risk. His wife might get raped and killed, his parents, his kids, his people will get killed and his way of life destroyed! Heaven is built for the coward, Reincarnation is for the warrior.

"HEAVEN VS REINCARNATION" BY DHARMA
ORDER ONLINE FROM BOOKSELLERS

Greed for the Easy Good Life

As I have noted before, Theists are stumped when asked what they will be doing in Heaven? Why would God need them in Heaven? What jobs does God need to get done that She needs human help? How much does it pay? Is it enough to live on? Or is Heaven like living in a Communist country, a house, a job are allotted and they all are alike and pay the same?

Religions are simply exploiting human greed, their frustration with life. What is the one big difference between real life and Heaven when it comes to living the easy good life? In real life no one is going to give you millions so that you can live the easy good life, but religions are more than happy to promise that "their" God will be more than happy to just GIVE. That's the operative word here, GIVE you the easy good life that you seek. In real life the good things in life have to be EARNED! Whether it is good grades or marks, a good job, starter on the sports team, a gold medal in the Olympics, a movie star, to be the next Einstein or the next Mozart, nothing is given! EARN, is the watchword and that is what we teach our kids. Sadly, when it comes to Heaven, greed takes over it seems. All the lessons that God has taught you through life are discarded, we drool over the lofty promises made by religious leaders, who are laughing at us behind our backs. Once more, we are the fools chasing after 'Fools Gold'!

Just because you don't like to study, dropping out of school won't make life better. Just because you hate your job, quitting won't make life better. You can dream all you want, hate life all you want, but death is not the gateway to a magic land of plenty.

"Heaven Vs Reincarnation"
By Dharma

Only Reincarnation can provide Justice

Open the newspaper or watch some news on TV and each and every day we get to read or watch about human lives being cut short. Some die due to natural disasters, others in accidents and others because of the evil in this world.

We have to ask, where is the Justice for these people, some die as young as a baby, lives cut short way too soon! The rest of us get to enjoy life in all its flavors. Have fun and play as little kids, loved and watched over by our parents, then school, friends, first dances, first crushes, hanging out in the mall, going to movies, college, a career, falling in love, getting married, kids, getting old and watching our kids grow up into adults, getting to be there when they celebrate their milestones, their birthdays, their weddings and finally a nice retired life.

But whether we live in the first or third, some of us never got to enjoy all that we have enjoyed. Will Heaven make up for all that? Of course not. If everyone ends up at the same place, we will all have our memories, our life experiences to look back on, but for some for whom the journey was stopped right at the beginning, they were cheated of life.

Only Reincarnation can provide Justice to such people. If they choose Life, REAL LIFE, they can come back and in another human life get to enjoy all that was denied to them in their previous life.

"Heaven Vs Reincarnation"
By Dharma

Morals matter, Ethics matter

There are quite a lot of people who will sell their souls and bodies in exchange for money, the easy life. Are you one of them? Even your own parents won't let you just sit on your lazy butt and do nothing! You are an adult, they may be a bit patient with you but at some point they will kick you out! As an adult, you are expected to get a job, stand on your own two feet and you are a child no more!

But there are quite a lot of people around this world who look for 'sugar daddies' to leech off. Men and Women sell their bodies, others take to flattery, some more become the henchmen for these rich and powerful people. Life is good for such people. They have sold their self-respect, their dignity, their souls in exchange for the easy good life.

Heaven is for such people. The selfish, the self-absorbed, only interested in self-gratification. God doesn't need you in Heaven, God is not going to let you just sit around in Heaven doing nothing for eternity. To even think that such a life is possible is shameful. Do the right thing.

"HEAVEN VS REINCARNATION" BY DHARMA

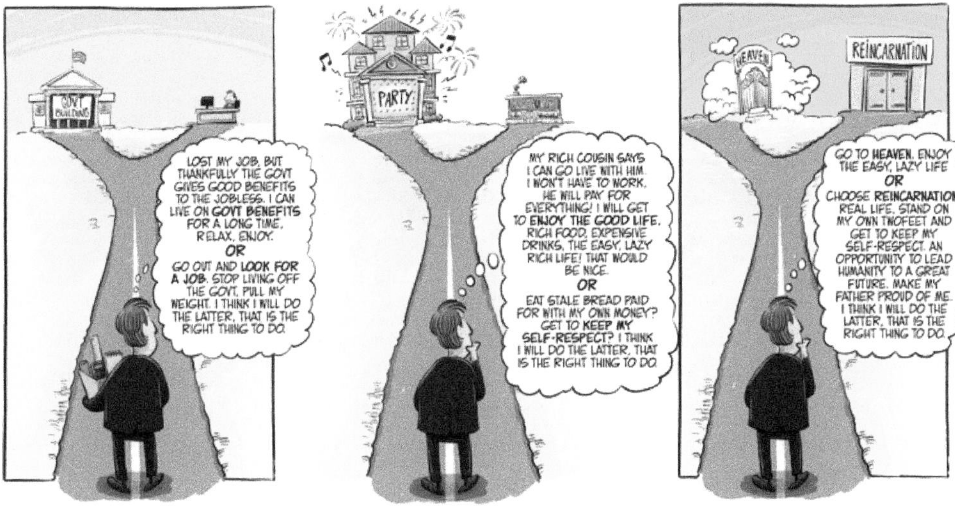
GOVT BUILDING
LOST MY JOB, BUT THANKFULLY THE GOVT GIVES GOOD BENEFITS TO THE JOBLESS. I CAN LIVE ON **GOVT BENEFITS** FOR A LONG TIME. RELAX, ENJOY. **OR** GO OUT AND **LOOK FOR A JOB**. STOP LIVING OFF THE GOVT, PULL MY WEIGHT. I THINK I WILL DO THE LATTER, THAT IS THE RIGHT THING TO DO.
PARTY
MY RICH COUSIN SAYS I CAN GO LIVE WITH HIM. I WON'T HAVE TO WORK. HE WILL PAY FOR EVERYTHING! I WILL GET TO **ENJOY THE GOOD LIFE**. RICH FOOD, EXPENSIVE DRINKS, THE EASY, LAZY RICH LIFE! THAT WOULD BE NICE. **OR** EAT STALE BREAD PAID FOR WITH MY OWN MONEY? GET TO **KEEP MY SELF-RESPECT**? I THINK I WILL DO THE LATTER, THAT IS THE RIGHT THING TO DO.
HEAVEN
REINCARNATION
GO TO **HEAVEN**. ENJOY THE EASY, LAZY LIFE **OR** CHOOSE **REINCARNATION**. REAL LIFE. STAND ON MY OWN TWOFEET AND GET TO KEEP MY SELF-RESPECT. AN OPPORTUNITY TO LEAD HUMANITY TO A GREAT FUTURE. MAKE MY FATHER PROUD OF ME. I THINK I WILL DO THE LATTER, THAT IS THE RIGHT THING TO DO.

Taking Responsibility for One's Actions

Every Hindu knows this rule, this teaching , you made the mess, it is your responsibility to clean it up. Your actions caused harm to innocent people, it is your responsibility to set things right. But you don't have to be a Hindu to know this truth. These are morals that you teach your kids.

If your kid, in a fit of anger upon losing a game, breaks his friend's toy, it is not enough for him to just cry a few tears in front of you. Yes, he is genuinely sorry for what he had done, but repentance is just the first step, not the last. A new toy has to be bought and delivered to the friend with a heart-felt apology. The cost of the new toy will either come out of your kid's allowance or he/she will be forced to do chores to make up the cost. As a parent it is your duty to teach your kid the right values and lessons.

I admit I am baffled when I hear about crying a few crocodile tears of repentance is enough for God. God will nicely forgive you and off you go enjoy Heaven. No need to apologize to the victim(s), no need to make up for the harm that you caused, crying a few tears takes under 2 minutes and you are done! How wonderful!

But is it?

God cannot teach you values. Evil people will do evil things, good people will continue to do good things. The moral will continue to do the right thing, the immoral will continue to take the easy way out and that is what religions promise, an easy way out. Shame on you for taking it, you shame God when you do that.

"Heaven Vs Reincarnation"
By Dharma

Religious Brain-Washing 2

Take a good look at the image. Don't you think the words are way too similar? What a sad statement that makes of us living in the modern and free world, that we continue to follow ideas from a primitive past. In the past people lived under Kings/Dictators/Strongmen and it was the prudent thing to do to keep one's head down, get down on one's knees before the King/Dictator/Strongman, swear one's loyalty to him and hope for a reward (Pascal's Wager). That was the life then.

Religions born from such days made God in such a Strongman's image - a King, like God sits on his throne in the Heavens, will reward his loyal followers(believers) and will punish the rest (unbelievers). No King could afford to have a disloyal person to remain in his kingdom back in those days. Today in our modern, free society, we can freely speak out against the President or Prime Minister, no one is kicking you out of the country for doing that.

But religions of today seem stuck in the past and sadly, so do seem the followers. All it takes to get the good life it seems is to grovel to the right Dictator. Polish the right shoes and get ahead. Atheists, Hindus, Buddhists and the like are polishing the wrong shoes, apparently, and will face unrelenting punishment. Sad, that even in the modern world, religions that preach collective condemnation and reward are the dominant ones.

What a sad statement to make of our educated, the intelligent, the media, the moral and ethical of this world.

"HEAVEN VS REINCARNATION" BY DHARMA

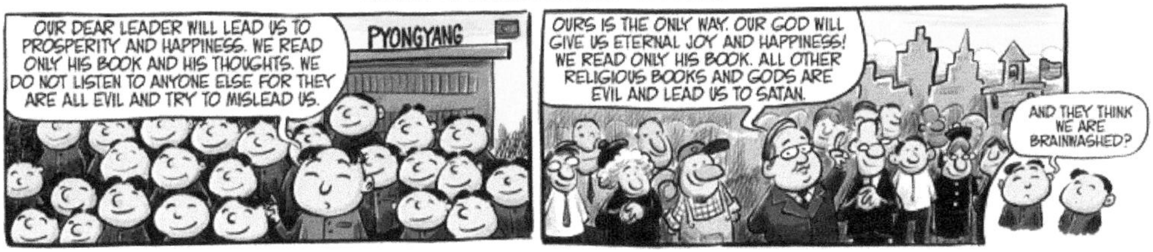

OUR DEAR LEADER WILL LEAD US TO PROSPERITY AND HAPPINESS. WE READ ONLY HIS BOOK AND HIS THOUGHTS. WE DO NOT LISTEN TO ANYONE ELSE FOR THEY ARE ALL EVIL AND TRY TO MISLEAD US.
PYONGYANG
OURS IS THE ONLY WAY. OUR GOD WILL GIVE US ETERNAL JOY AND HAPPINESS! WE READ ONLY HIS BOOK. ALL OTHER RELIGIOUS BOOKS AND GODS ARE EVIL AND LEAD US TO SATAN.
AND THEY THINK WE ARE BRAINWASHED?

Our Morals are Flexible

Take a good look at the image. It has always puzzled me why the first three are condemned, correctly of course, while the fourth gets a free pass! In fact, it is actively promoted! Plenty of letters, articles and editorials condemning all kinds of division and hate, all kinds of discrimination whether it be racism, sexism, ageism, Casteism and what not. But the number of letters, articles and editorials that condemn Religious-Apartheid being actively promoted by the dominant religions is zero! Yes, Zero!

Over the years no one has ever asked what kind of a God would divide people based simply on their religious affiliation! Does God not care for us as individual human beings? What we did in life does not matter? All that matters to God is whether we support him or not by making sure we join the "right" religion? And how are we to know which religion is the right one? Almost all religions have the blood of innocents on their hands. Are these the religions that claim to speak for God?

Such brutality is reflected in their threats. Their God is no better than a Hitler! Hitler only saw the Jewish person for his religion. He did not see the human being, an old man who had worked tirelessly for the betterment of Germany all his life suddenly found himself boarding a rail car bound for gas chambers along with his little grandchild!

Such will the fate of billions of Hindus, Buddhists and Atheists! We too are bound for gas chambers in Hell!

I don't know which is harder to take, the abuse from such religions or the silence from the moral and educated.

"Heaven Vs Reincarnation"
By Dharma

Do Animals Go to Heaven?

As an animal lover, I have to laugh at our arrogance. Some religious people say animals do not have a soul and they do not go to Heaven. But we do? We have souls? We, who continue to brutalize this planet and all the other creatures living in it, we deserve to be rewarded with the easy good life? While animals that suffered at our hands will continue to suffer even in the afterlife?

It shows clearly how fake Heaven is. It's just a feel good fantasy to make ourselves happy. It first started in cave man days when the little child asked her father why grandma is not waking up or answering her. What does a dad supposed to say? But of course, "Grandma is now in a better place"

Religions have been using this concept ever since. What is sad is that we seem so oblivious to the pain and suffering that we cause to animals and yet think that we deserve to be rewarded with a life where there is no pain or suffering. A joyful life in the company of our loved ones and friends.

But such dreams will come true, reborn as a plant, a tree, or even a bug. We will be with our loved ones. With no brain to speak of, we will know no pain or suffering. With no concept of time, we will live "forever"

"HEAVEN VS REINCARNATION" BY DHARMA
ORDER ONLINE FROM BOOKSELLERS

HEAVEN

THE WOMB, CHILDHOOD, THE PAST, COWARD, FLIGHT, SELFISH, RETIRE, EXIST, WEAK, SHAMELESS, TAKER, SAVED, ANIMAL, BEG, HAND-OUT, FOOLISH, LOWER, UNCARING, JOY AND HAPPINESS, FANTASY

REINCARNATION

LIFE, ADULTHOOD, THE FUTURE, WARRIOR, FIGHT, CARING, WORK, LIVE, STRONG, SELF-RESPECT, GIVER, SAVIOR, HUMAN, EARN, HAND-UP, WISE, HIGHER, CARING, PAIN AND SUFFERING, REAL LIFE!

Do not Kneel to God

When was the last time you knelt before anyone? Who kneels anymore? But it used to happen quite a lot in the past, did it not? Images of subjects kneeling before their master, the King. Subjects were expected to do that, show their loyalty, show that they were good slaves and servants ready to blindly obey their master.

Decide whom you want to be - a 'Child of God' or a 'Slave/Servant'?

The 4 top religions of today can be classified into two categories, Christianity and Islam view God as a Master/King, hence lots of getting down on one's knees and bowing to the Master. A servant may serve only one Master, hence the one God. Hinduism and Buddhism view God as a parent/teacher. In life, many a teacher, and many parents, which is where the maxim comes from; "It takes a village to raise a child". Most Hindus remain standing or sit in the temple and a few kneel to God.

How you view yourself will decide your responsibilities and duties. As a slave you blindly obey, as a 'Child of God' your rights and responsibilities are different. Imagine a rich man with grown kids helping him in his business. This rich man also employs a few servants. One day disaster strikes, a natural disaster wipes out all that the rich man owns! Heartsick, the once rich man ends up in the hospital, broken and dying. Where are the servants? Long gone! Servants stick around only as long as times are good (Heaven), but it is up to the sons and daughters to hold the old man's hand, tell him that everything will be all right, that they will take care of him now and pay the hospital bills and care for their father. Those are the rights and responsibilities of a 'Child of God'. We stick through thick and thin, not just when times are good. Our place is right here on this Earth, in the REAL WORLD! Please do not shame God by lowering yourself down to a 'Slave/Servant'.

"HEAVEN VS REINCARNATION" BY DHARMA
ORDER ONLINE FROM BOOKSELLERS

Get the Good Life the Easy Way

Life has been so hard for so long that it is natural for humans to want some joy and happiness in their lives. Today, for those of us lucky to live in the first world, we do enjoy the easy good life but for the vast majority of humanity life is a daily struggle. Life was much, much worse in the past as most depended on agriculture to make a living. Considered the world's hardest job even today, little law and order and of course primitive medicine meant watching their loved ones die right before their eyes.

Life was "solitary, poor, nasty, brutish and short"(Hobbes) and naturally people loved the idea of a God who would nicely take them in and give them an easy and endless good life. Back then most work was primitive and all one needed was enough muscle. Most jobs were given based on good contacts. Life was easier on those close to the rich and powerful. It paid to get down on one's knees and swear loyalty to the powerful and hope for a reward (Pascal's Wager).

That was life then, much has changed since then, but sadly, religions continue to remain stuck in the primitive past. Today, in most western countries, it takes certain skills to get a job or a promotion or a contract. The good life is EARNED, not given. But there are still pockets of such primitive ways in Communist and Dictator-ruled countries , where Jobs, promotions and contracts are handed over based on whom-you-, now and not what-you-know.

What is pathetic is to see the world's dominant religions subscribing to such wicked ways.

Heaven Vs Reincarnation
by Dharma

You Get what you Pay For

One of the arguments that I make in my book is that you can't fool God. You can't get something for nothing. Expecting to find gold in a garage sale box marked "free" is foolish. God, through the medium of life has taught you that nothing good in life will come without a struggle, falling down several times, failing endlessly but one must keep getting up. Quitters don't get rewarded. No pain, No Gain! Such lessons are self-evident.

But the opposite is exactly what religions promise us. Quit! Quit on life and God will reward you with the easy good life in Heaven! As you can see from the image, they are in for a surprise. Nietzsche, was the one western philosopher who read Hindu texts and understood what they were trying to teach. That our choice must be to keep moving forward, never settle for living in the past. There is more to life than simple pleasures of the glesh -the 3 S's - safety, sex and sustenance. Animals get that and those who run after Heaven will end up regretting their choice.

"HEAVEN VS REINCARNATION" BY DHARMA

ORDER ONLINE FROM BOOKSELLERS

HEAVEN

THE WOMB, CHILDHOOD,
THE PAST, COWARD,
FLIGHT, SELFISH, RETIRE,
EXIST, WEAK, SHAMELESS,

TAKER, SAVED, ANIMAL,
BEG, HAND-OUT, FOOLISH,
LOWER, UNCARING, JOY
AND HAPPINESS, FANTASY

REINCARNATION

LIFE, ADULTHOOD,
THE FUTURE, WARRIOR,
FIGHT, CARING, WORK,
LIVE, STRONG, SELF-RESPECT,

GIVER, SAVIOR, HUMAN,
EARN, HAND-UP, WISE,
HIGHER, CARING, PAIN
AND SUFFERING, REAL LIFE!

DIFFERENCE BETWEEN HEAVEN AND MOKSHA, DIFFERENCE BETWEEN PLEASURES OF THE FLESH AND SOUL

Do You Care?

We all have heard of religious people talk about how in Heaven we will be with all our loved ones, that life will be full of joy and happiness. Ever hear of them mention the loved ones we will leave behind? What if you are the bread-winner of the family? How will your family get on without your help? So then, in Heaven, do you not care anymore?

Children get lost, some are abducted - are the dead grandparents and parents enjoying cake in Heaven? A child lost in the forest is hungry, tired, crying for his mommy as he lies down to sleep, perhaps for the last time. Total strangers are spending endless hours helping search for him (that could be you if you choose Reincarnation) and the kids own loved ones are taking in a ball game in Heaven?

So many bad things happen in this world. Terrorism, disease, violence, discrimination, the list of horrors is endless. Does being in Heaven means that one will stop caring? It seems that way, does it not?

Let's get this straight, if Heaven exists and it is a wonderful and joyful place, it is such a place before you got there, it will be while you are there, and guess what, it will still be a wonderful and joyful place if you choose to leave. No one will miss you, no one will care!

But it is down on Earth that you are needed and wanted, the place where you will be missed, where people care. I keep saying, God is down here with us, with loving, caring people.

"HEAVEN VS REINCARNATION" BY DHARMA

HEAVEN		REINCARNATION	
THE WOMB, CHILDHOOD, THE PAST, COWARD, FLIGHT, **SELFISH**, RETIRE, EXIST, WEAK, SHAMELESS,	TAKER, SAVED, ANIMAL, BEG, HAND-OUT, FOOLISH, LOWER, UNCARING, JOY AND HAPPINESS, FANTASY	LIFE, ADULTHOOD, THE FUTURE, WARRIOR, FIGHT, **CARING**, WORK, LIVE, STRONG, SELF-RESPECT,	GIVER, SAVIOR, HUMAN, EARN, HAND-UP, WISE, HIGHER, CARING, PAIN AND SUFFERING, **REAL LIFE!**

So Many Questions, No Answers -
But Where Are The Questions?

I started this journey with a logical, reasoning mind. Giving myself harsh answers first, there is no evidence of God or any Heavens or Hells or Reincarnation. All the ideas of God came from earth, with earth-bound people elevated to a God level. The "Abrahamic God" is none other than a local King/Dictator/Strongman stands out like a sore thumb! Just like a Dictator who would reward his loyal supporters and have his doubters killed or kicked out off his country, so does this God! Heaven is for his loyal believers only, the rest of us are condemned to eternal torture! And yet, even in the modern age, so few seem to see through this facade of religion.

Here I ask some more questions and religious people use the same tactic, the same opium, the same Kool-Aid to shut up all doubters and it has worked wonderfully over the centuries. What is sad that even the best of minds seems to fall for this easy trick. No wonder religion has been compared to an Opium.

"HEAVEN VS. REINCARNATION" BY DHARMA

ORDER ONLINE FROM BOOKSELLERS

HEAVEN

THE WOMB, CHILDHOOD, THE PAST, COWARD, FIGHT, SELFISH, RETIRE, EXIST, WEAK, SHAMELESS, TAKER, SAVED, ANIMAL, BEG, HAND-OUT, FOOLISH, LOWER, JOY AND HAPPINESS, FANTASY

REINCARNATION

LIFE, ADULTHOOD, THE FUTURE, WARRIOR, FIGHT, CARING, ASPIRE, LIVE, STRONG, SELF-RESPECT, GIVER, SAVIOR, HUMAN, EARN, HAND-UP, WISE, HIGHER, PAIN AND SUFFERING, REAL LIFE!

WHAT DOES ONE *DO* IN HEAVEN? WHAT JOBS ARE AVAILABLE? WHAT DOES THE MAKER OF THIS VAST UNIVERSE HAVE FOR US TO DO? IF THERE ARE NO JOBS, DO WE JUST FLOAT AROUND DOING NOTHING FOR ETERNITY?

I AM THE BREAD-WINNER OF MY FAMILY. HOW WILL THEY GET ON WITHOUT ME? HOW AM I SUPPOSED TO ENJOY HEAVEN KNOWING THAT MY FAMILY IS SUFFERING DOWN ON EARTH?

IF MY SON MADE A MISTAKE, I HAVE TAUGHT HIM TO NOT ONLY APOLOGIZE, BUT TO ALSO MAKE GOOD THE LOSS. INSTEAD, HE CAN SNEAK OUT THE BACK DOOR WITH JUST A FEW TEARS OF REPENTANCE? ARE THESE THE MORALS THAT WE SHOULD BE TEACHING OUR KIDS?

WHY WORRY ABOUT ALL THAT? HERE, DRINK THIS OPIUM OF HEAVEN! ENJOY!

GIMME!

GIMME!

GIMME!

AND THEY THINK WE ARE BRAINWASHED?

Our Morals are Flexible

No writer or editor will never make the mistake of not calling Hitler pure evil. 1515, also, rightly called malevolent, wicked and immoral. What was their evil crime? They did not see people as individual human beings, each one of us different from the other. They collectively condemned an entire group of people based solely on their religious affiliation.

A Jewish citizen of Germany, who had spent his entire life working for the betterment of Germany, suddenly found himself, in his old age, being bundled into a rail car along with his 10-year-old grandson, destined for the gas chambers

1515 used to line up non-Muslims and gave them a choice - convert or die! Some did not even get that choice, they not being Muslims, meant a death sentence for them. Back in the day, plenty of people were killed in the name of religion, Islam spread by the sword. Mexicans, conquered by the Spanish, were given the same option - convert to the new religion of their Masters or die! Christians were the 1515 back in the day!

While the above two are, rightly, condemned, the ideas that gave birth to them are actually promoted! Religious division and hate actively preached while the media, the educated and the moral look the other way!

"HEAVEN VS REINCARNATION" BY DHARMA
ORDER ONLINE FROM BOOKSELLERS

HEAVEN

THE WOMB, CHILDHOOD, THE PAST, COWARD, FLIGHT, SELFISH, RETIRE, EXIST, WEAK, SHAMELESS,

TAKER, SAVED, ANIMAL, BEG, HAND-OUT, FOOLISH, LOWER, UNCARING, JOY AND HAPPINESS, FANTASY

REINCARNATION

LIFE, ADULTHOOD, THE FUTURE, WARRIOR, FIGHT, CARING, WORK, LIVE, STRONG, SELF-RESPECT,

GIVER, SAVIOR, HUMAN, EARN, HAND-UP, WISE, HIGHER, CARING, PAIN AND SUFFERING, REAL LIFE!

The Purpose & Meaning of Life

We all wonder at one time or another about this topic, do we not? According to the major religions the purpose of life is to make sure we join the "right" religion, pray to the "right" God so that he will be pleased and will reward us.

So, basically the purpose of life is to make sure we polish the right shoes to get the good life? It made a lot of sense back in the day when people lived under Kings, brutal Dictators and Strongmen and it paid to pledge loyalty and obedience to the powerful. But that is the past, today we don't live like that but yet.. ...

"HEAVEN VS. REINCARNATION" BY DHARMA
ORDER ONLINE FROM BOOKSELLERS

HEAVEN
THE WOMB, CHILDHOOD, THE PAST,
COWARD, FIGHT, SELFISH, RETIRE,
EXIST, WEAK, SHAMELESS, TAKER,
SAVED, ANIMAL, BEG, HAND-OUT,
FOOLISH, LOWER, JOY AND
HAPPINESS, FANTASY

REINCARNATION
LIFE, ADULTHOOD, THE FUTURE,
WARRIOR, FIGHT, CARING, ASPIRE,
LIVE, STRONG, SELF-RESPECT,
GIVER, SAVIOR, HUMAN, EARN,
HAND-UP, WISE, HIGHER, PAIN
AND SUFFERING, REAL LIFE!

TODAY IS YOUR LUCKY DAY, TODAY I WILL TEACH YOU THE PURPOSE AND MEANING OF LIFE. IT IS PRETTY SIMPLE. MAKE SURE YOU JOIN THE 'RIGHT' RELIGION AND PRAY TO THE 'RIGHT' GOD. THEN YOU WILL BE REWARDED WITH THE GOOD LIFE. GOD FORBID IF YOU ARE AN ATHEIST OR BELONG TO THE 'WRONG' RELIGION, YOU WILL BE BRUTALIZED ENDLESSLY.

MORALS AND ETHICS 101

BUT SIR, PLENTY OF GOOD PEOPLE COME FROM ALL WALKS OF LIFE. ARE WE SAYING WHAT WE DO IN LIFE DOES NOT MATTER? THE BUDDHA, GANDHIJI, EINSTEIN, PLATO AND MANY MORE WHO HAVE CONTRIBUTED SO MUCH TO OUR WORLD ARE BURNING IN HELL? WHEREAS RAPISTS, MURDERERS OF THE 'RIGHT' RELIGION CAN REPENT THEIR WAY TO HEAVEN? MORALS AND PRINCIPLES DO NOT MATTER?

THESE ARE THE DOMINANT IDEAS OF TODAY. THE NUMBER OF STUDENTS LIKE YOURSELF WHO HAVE ASKED SUCH QUESTIONS ARE FEW AND FAR BETWEEN AND PROFESSORS LIKE MYSELF ARE FEWER STILL. CONVERSIONS AROUND THE WORLD ARE DRIVEN BY SUBJECTING THE POOR AND UNEDUCATED TO SUCH INDUCEMENTS AND THREATS. THE SILENCE OF THE EDUCATED AND MORAL MAKES SUCH ABUSE POSSIBLE.

God is my Ticket to the Easy Good Life in Heaven

We see so many people selling their souls, basically, supporting evil strong men, become his henchmen, beat up his enemies, kill innocents by his say-so. They do it so that they are rewarded by the Strong man, the easy life is theirs.

Others make friends with the rich, hoping he or she will take them to expensive restaurants and night-clubs, vacations - live the good life at the rich person's expense. When I hear talk about Heaven, I hear the same words - "This God will give us the good life. We should pray to him so that he will be pleased and will reward us".

Our views of God have remained at this shallow level even today in the 21st century. Doesn't say much about us, does it?

"Heaven Vs Reincarnation"
By Dharma

Heaven
The Womb, Childhood, the Past, Coward, Flight, Selfish, Retire, Exist, Weak, Shameless, Taker, Saved, Animal, Beg, Hand-out, Foolish, Lower, Joy and Happiness, Fantasy.

Reincarnation
Life, Adulthood, the Future, Warrior, Fight, Caring, Work, Live, Strong, Self-Respect, Giver, Savior, Human, Earn, Hand-Up, Wise, Higher, Pain and Suffering, REAL LIFE!

GOD IS MY TICKET TO THE EASY GOOD LIFE, MY SUGAR DADDY.

The King and the Teacher

The four major religions can be categorized into two King/Master religions -Christianity and Islam. The Parent/Teacher faiths - Hinduism & Buddhism. King/Master religions are quite simple. You pray to the King/Master and he will reward you. The goal is the easy good life in Heaven and to get there one must pray to the right God. Just as in the olden days when living under a strong and just King made all the difference . Life was different then and religions reflected those times.

Parent/Teacher faiths are far more complex. There is no reward as such. Life itself, the journey, is its own reward. The goal is enlightenment and knowledge. To become a Buddha. Actions matter, not religion! To become the savior, not the saved. To become the warrior, not the coward and to aspire, not retire.

"Heaven Vs Reincarnation" By Dharma

HEAVEN

THE WOMB, CHILDHOOD, THE PAST, COWARD, FLIGHT, SELFISH, RETIRE, EXIST, WEAK, SHAMELESS, TAKER, SAVED, ANIMAL, BEG, HAND-OUT, FOOLISH, LOWER, JOY AND HAPPINESS, FANTASY

REINCARNATION

LIFE, ADULTHOOD, THE FUTURE, WARRIOR, FIGHT, CARING, ASPIRE, LIVE, STRONG, SELF-RESPECT, GIVER, SAVIOR, HUMAN, EARN, HAND-UP, WISE, HIGHER, PAIN AND SUFFERING, REAL LIFE!

King/Master Religions

GET DOWN ON OUR KNEES AND PRAY TO THE KING/MASTER AND BE REWARDED, ONLY THE LOYAL WILL BE REWARDED, EXCLUSIVE, COMMUNIST RELIGIONS, ACTIONS, MORALS AND ETHICS DO NOT MATTER, THE OPERATIVE WORD IS BEG & THE REWARD IS HEAVEN - A RETIREMENT HOME - PLEASURES OF THE FLESH

Parent/Teacher Faiths

MAKE GOD PROUD, THE GOAL IS ENLIGHTENMENT, BECOME A BUDDHA, THE NEXT EINSTEIN, THE NEXT MOZART, ACTIONS ARE ALL THAT MATTERS, INCLUSIVE, DEMOCRATIC FAITHS, THE OPERATIVE WORD IS EARN, THE "REWARD" IS WORK, MOKSHA - PLEASURES OF THE HEART, MIND AND SOUL

Heaven is for the Old, the Retired, whereas Reincarnation is for the Young, the Dreamer

We have asked this question before, "What does one DO in Heaven?" Heaven seems to be a nice retirement home. Billions of people floating around, staring at each other, bored out of their skulls. They exist, they do not live. Yes, God's Grand Plan! Indeed.

Life, REAL LIFE, awaits those who choose Reincarnation. One day humans will colonize this galaxy, will travel the stars! One day the life depicted in the Star Wars movies will become a reality. And those who choose Reincarnation will enjoy the world of the future. They will build such a world! And it will make God proud!

"HEAVEN VS REINCARNATION" BY DHARMA
ORDER ONLINE FROM BOOKSELLERS

HEAVEN

THE WOMB, CHILDHOOD, **THE PAST**, COWARD, FLIGHT, SELFISH, **RETIRE**, EXIST, WEAK, SHAMELESS,

TAKER, SAVED, ANIMAL, BEG, HAND-OUT, FOOLISH, LOWER, UNCARING, JOY AND HAPPINESS, FANTASY

REINCARNATION

LIFE, ADULTHOOD, **THE FUTURE**, WARRIOR, FIGHT, CARING, **WORK**, LIVE, STRONG, SELF-RESPECT,

GIVER, SAVIOR, HUMAN, EARN, HAND-UP, WISE, HIGHER, CARING, PAIN AND SUFFERING, REAL LIFE!

Heaven is a metaphor for the womb, childhood and the past. A yearning to go back to the wonderful days of our childhood. A time of zero worries or responsibilities, loved ones watching over us, protecting us, giving us love and affection. We were fed, clothed, shielded from the perils of life, basically we got to live in a bubble. Reincarnation then, stands for life, adulthood and the future. We cannot turn the clock back, we cannot live in the past, running away from real life is not the answer. We MUST move out of the nest and face life head-on. The future life depicted in the Star Wars movies will become a reality one day but it won't build itself. We must work, sacrifice, make the right choices so that the future dream world will come true. Those who choose Reincarnation, real life over a fantasy retirement home in the sky, will enjoy the fruits of the coming future world!

Author Dharma would love to hear your thoughts.

You can contact him at: HeavenVsReincarnation@Yahoo.com

Ingram Content Group UK Ltd.
Milton Keynes UK
UKHW051924230523
422240UK00004B/58

9 781912 850334